Building the Road to Success

By Jorge Fernandez de Cordova

Published by
Jorge Fernandez de Cordova
Fontana, CA

ISBN
978-0-6151-5491-6

SUCCESS

Some People Dream of Success,

While Other People Live to Crush

Those Dreams

Congratulations on the purchase of this book. You are about to start an adventure which will reward you for the rest of your life.....

Have you been in situations where you seem to be going nowhere, feel inadequate and unable to face life with enthusiasm and confidence, *this book is just for you.* If you are disgusted with mediocrity and not content to just drift through life, these pages will offer you an alternative.

Please make yourself open and receptive to new concepts, values and beliefs, and you will discover the greatness inside of you.

When you learn to reorganize your thought process, you will awaken THE NEW YOU.

It makes no difference who you are, which background you are coming from, what education level you have, what your life situation is, YOU can become successful and unleash your greatness.

This book is dedicated to my family:
My loving wife, Blanca, my awesome son, Jorge,
and my future Baby Girl America who's on the way.

8

ACKNOWLEDGEMENTS

I want to start off first by thanking GOD my lord and savior, because without him I would not be here writing this book, I also want to thank my wife, Blanca, and my son, Jorge.

Thank you for allowing me the space to do what I came here to do. I'd also like to thank my parents, Jorge and Linda, as well as my sisters, Erika and Pamela, and my brother, Hector, for your unending love and support.

It would be difficult to acknowledge everyone from whom I have borrowed ideas but I insist on thanking a few by name.

I want to thank my mentors, Mike Litman, Brian Litman, Art Williams, Hector La Marque for their excellent work in helping others to achieve their goals.

Dr. Robert Anthony for his outstanding programs and booklets on self-improvement; and the writings of Napoleon Hill, Ralph Waldo Emerson, and many more Successful people whom I have learned so much.

TABLE OF CONTENTS

INTRODUCTION

My Story

I want to tell you my story, where I come from, and where I am today.

I was raised and born in Mexico City, Mexico. I went to school, graduated from high school, and I had just started my career in the Medical Field. At that point in my life I knew that what I wanted to do was to help people. I wasn't sure if the medical field would fit me, but I wanted to help. I studied 6 months of Medicine, and then something came to my mind that I felt I had to do, and that was the fact that I wanted to learn English.

One of the major reasons to learn English was, because the majority of medicine books are written in English, and I wanted to be able to understand it without struggle.

I had an idea; I have relatives who live in California. So I thought to myself "if I can convince my Dad to let me go for a year and learn the language, that would be awesome" My plans were to learn English go back to Mexico, finish my career in Medicine and do my specialty in United States. I figured if by then I speak the language, and I should have no problem.

Finally, after a lot of asking to my Dad, he let me go, we talked to our relatives to let me stayed for a year, they agreed and there I go. May 1999 I was flying thousands and thousands of miles away from home.

I came to United States, and first thing was first. I had to find a job. So I did, I started working at a fast food restaurant as a cook. The job was good, but I knew that is not what I wanted to do for life, so I stayed there for about 11 months before I joined the Service.

When I was 14 years old, one of my dreams was to become a United States Marine. Little by little I was approaching my goal, I was living in United States, and all I needed to find was a recruiting station.

I met my wife at work (actually she was my boss. Well, ok she still is) and to my luck, her brother was a Marine. I said "Yes" I knew that if I could talk to him about getting involved, he would tell me where the recruiting office was.

I did, went to see the recruiter and in a matter of minutes, I was taking my test to get qualified. Of course at that point I didn't speak much English, but my DESIRE to learn the language and to become a Marine was nothing but a challenge, and I was up for the challenge.

I took my test, I passed, and a week later my recruiter tells me that I have been accepted, I had to do only one more test and that was at The Military Entrance Processing Station (MEPS) where I had to do my final processing and a medical examination, and I was leaving in 2 weeks to boot camp.

I had to take a quick vacation to Mexico City and let my parents know I was leaving to the military. I never got the approval from my parents to do what I wanted to do. I'm sure the news came like a hook to the liver, but I had to do it, something inside of me was burning in desire to join the Service.

My parents were shocked at first, they told me "We don't agree, but if that's what you want to do, go ahead, you have our blessing." That was the best moment of my life.

Now it was time to fly back and get everything ready to go to MEPS.

While I was taking my medical examination, one of the doctors that was checking my vitals, try to start a conversation with me, obviously, I couldn't understand a word he said. The few English I knew, I could understand what he told me then "What service are you joining?" I told him the Marines. You should have seen the look in his face, his eyes popped out of his face and his mouth dropped, and then he told me "Good luck boy, I don't think you are going to survive."

I knew he was wrong, how could I not survive my dream.

The whole process was over and there you have me, doing the military oath, just repeating what I was hearing, I never knew what I was getting into, until I got to boot camp in May of 2000.

My time in boot camp was very pleasant (Oh yeah!!) I had Drill Instructors yelling at us, and teaching us how to become Marines, but I had no clue. I was living my dream, but I couldn't understand a word.

If I wouldn't have the burning desire to become a Marine, I would of probably had quitted long before starting. What I did instead of running away, I told my wife (she was my girlfriend at that time) to send me a dictionary. One way or another I had to figure out the way to learn and show everyone who didn't believe I could do it, that they were wrong. By the way it took me 3 months to learn English (Every time I could I was reading my dictionary learning something new).

I graduated in August of 2000. I did everything I had to do, attended schools, training and finally got my Duty Station in Camp Pendleton, CA, in December of 2000.

In April of 2001, I was transferred to another company within the same battalion.

In August of 2001, I was deployed for the first time, I was living my dream, I had earned the title Marine, got my specialty as a Gunsmith, was assigned to my duty station and now I'm going in a 6 months deployment.

During my deployment, unfortunately, the twin towers were hit and it was time for us to prepare for what was about to happened. We went to war to Afghanistan. Our 6 months deployment turned to be 7 months and with countless experiences.

In the middle of all this I was doing what I wanted to do, HELP OTHERS, what a great way to help other than serving my country with pride and honor.

We came back and a few months later I was sent to Iraq in January of 2003, for a period of 5 months, and while all this was going on, my wife was pregnant of my beautiful son. What a challenge leave my spouse in the time she needed me the most, but I had no choice.

You know the rest of what happened in Iraq.

Today, I own 3 businesses, and there's nothing that can prevent me from achieving my goals.

What I'm trying to say with my story is that, it doesn't matter who you are, what past you may have, what life situation you are in, you can ACHIEVE your goals. Once you have the desire and focus everyday on accomplishing your goals, there's nothing and no one who can stop you, but many people are afraid to change.

Change is a natural thing, and is a fundamental part of life. Without change, where would this world be?

MONKEY BUSINESS

"If you don't make a change, your life will be the same forever…."
-Dr. Robert Anthony

A group of scientists, decided to make an experiment on behavior. They put 5 monkeys in a cage, a ladder, and hanging from the top of the cage was a bunch of bananas.

After a while the monkeys started to get hungry, so one of them figure out how to open the ladder and placed it right below the bananas.

Every time a monkey tried to get on the ladder to eat the bananas, the scientists will throw cold water at the monkeys. Then another monkey try to get on the ladder again, and again the scientists threw cold water at them. It went on and on until the monkeys were too afraid of getting even close to the ladder.

Then the scientists decided to place a brand new monkey to the cage and withdraw one of the veterans there. After some time, the new monkey started to get hungry and tried to get the bunch of bananas, but right before he got to it, the other monkeys pulled him down and started to punch him. Obviously the new monkey was freaking out, since he didn't know what hit him. So then he tries again, and once again the other monkeys pull him down and start punching him until the monkey wouldn't get close anymore.

So then they put another monkey in the cage, after a while the monkey gets hungry and tries to get to the ladder and right before he gets there, the prior monkey grabs him and all of them started punching him (I guess the prior monkey thought it was a good time for payback) so then he tried again, and once again until he learned the lesson.

The plan went on, until the scientists replaced all monkeys, now they had a cage full of new monkeys, and every time a monkey will get close to the ladder, the other monkeys will grab him and started to punch the new guy.

The conclusion was. The new monkeys didn't know the reason behind the old monkeys of getting close to the ladder. They never knew about the cold water. All they knew was that if you get close to that ladder, you will get punched, but didn't know why?

Well many of us act the same way, we do things a certain way without really knowing the real reason behind it.

Another story is the one about a girl that every time she will cook turkey, will cut the turkey in pieces, put it in a tray and straight to the oven. When she was asked why she did it that way, she would answer "That's the way my mother always did it."

Next, the mother was asked the same question, why does she cut the turkey before cooking it. Her reply was "That's the way my mother always did it."

Now, the grandmother was asked why did she cut the turkey before cooking it, and her reply was surprising. She said "Well the reason is simple, my oven was too small, and that was the only way to fit it in."

Surprisingly enough, we do a lot of things because we think that's the way things should be done without really knowing the real reason behind it.

The monkeys didn't have to start fighting each other to grab a banana. They didn't know about the cold water. The girl could have cooked her turkey whole if she knew the real reason why her grandmother cooked it that way.

So take a close look at your ways of doing things and ask yourself if that's the only way to do it, or why you family has done a certain thing the same way through generations.

ARE YOU IMPRISONED BY YOUR BELIEFS?

"Some things have to be believed to be seen…."
-Ralph Hodgson

What are beliefs? Just put it this way, they are the conscious and unconscious information we have accepted to be true, and this form the basis for our behavior.

Our beliefs imprison us and deny us access to what is *REAL*. We see only *what we want,* and reject everything else.

Truth can never be revealed to the so-called "firm-believer." The type of person who is always quoting "facts." He does not want to recognize anything outside his beliefs, and everything seems to be a threat and obviously he disagrees to.

He goes through life labeling everything that is new or different as "evil" or "unacceptable," and everything that is old and traditional as "good." He can not understand that Truth, *no matter how painful*, is always by its very nature, "good," and that a lie, *regardless of how much we are in love with it,* it's always, by its very nature, "bad."

The person who is a "firm believer" has no option to change his mind. This makes him ignorant .He can only recognize what lies within his beliefs.

If you want to make a change in your life, you must first understand the root of your problems. This lies in your "mistaken certainties."

Mistaken Certainties are things you are sure to be true but which, in fact, are not. They are based on wishful thinking which distorts reality and leads to self-deception.

We want things to be as we would like them to be rather than accept them as they are. You can only change the world to the extent that you can change *yourself,* and you can only change yourself to the degree that you become aware of your mistaken certainties.

Emerson said, "We are what we think about all day long." Everything that is happening to you right now in your mental, physical, emotional and spiritual world is the result of what is going on in your mind.

Let's face it! We all find it difficult to change our present level of awareness.

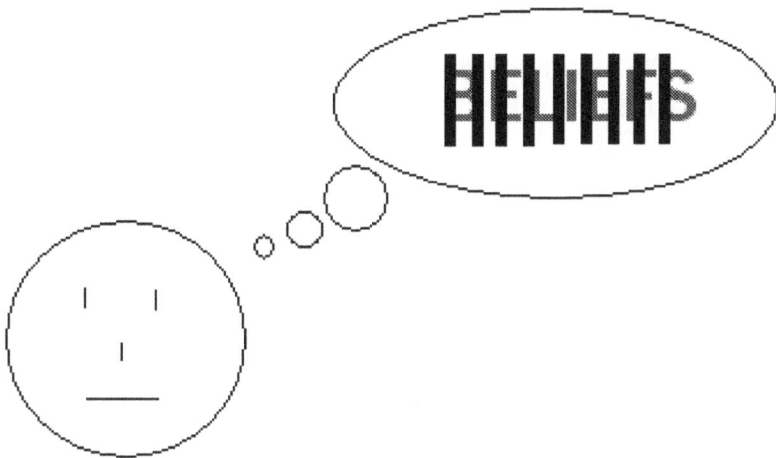

UNLEASH THE POWER TO CHANGE.

Once, William Shakespeare said, "We know what we are, but not what we may be."

Is this you? How long on a day you spend concentrating on your limitations, your failures, your blundering way of doing things, seldom stopping to think of what you might be?

The problem here starts all the way back from your childhood. You have been condition by false concepts, values and beliefs which have been holding you from finding out how talented and unique you are.

The good news is that you are the co-creator of your life, and as such you have the power to change anything you don't like. Every Successful person knows that you cannot look to someone outside yourself to solve your problems.

Buddha said, "Be a lamp unto your own feet and do not seek outside yourself." You posses self-healing powers to health, happiness, abundance and peace of mind once you break the bonds of negative thinking.

Disassociate from negative people. Any one, who tries to stop you and tries to hold you back, does not want you to succeed.

Nothing will change until you do. Change starts with you wanting to change.

I want to make a pause here and ask you if you are ready to change. I want to warn you that change is not easy, and most times is not pleasant, but without stretching yourself it will be no growth.

"If you do what others won't, you will get what others won't…"

This is totally up to you.

STOP PLEASING OTHERS.

Bill Cosby once said, "I don't know the secret to success, but the secret to failure is trying to please others."

Do you try to please others? Do you worry about what people will say or will talk about you? Are you trying to make others happy with your decisions?

"If you don't design your own life plan, chances are you'll fall into someone else's plan. And guess what they may have planned for you? Not much."
--Jim Rohn

If you don't have a clear goal of what you want, or what you want to do, chances are that you will end up working for someone who does have a goal.

Stop trying to please others, and save the world without….

Saving yourself FIRST!

Read that again.

You have to help yourself first. Clean your own backyard first before you start cleaning the neighbor's.

It is not your job to please others no matter who may have told you that.

Many people use the philosophy of helping others first as an escape from taking responsibility for changing their lives. They say things like "My husband or wife must come first, boyfriends or girlfriends; churches or families or simply that the world must come first."

Don't do that, don't run away from your responsibilities. Your own welfare should be first. Do you know what doctors do when there's a disaster such as an earthquake, etc? They are the first ones out of the building. Why?

Why don't they save the patients first? Why don't they get the other people out of the building first? Why?

Well, simple. They are no good dead or trapped inside a crumbled building. By saving themselves first, they can help other people.

This is just how life works, don't try to figure out more. That's it.

You help more people by helping yourself first.

YOUR HABITS WILL DETERMINE YOUR FUTURE.

You might not be aware of this, but your habits will play a big role in the creation of your life.

Let me start off by defining habits.

What are Habits?

Habits are something you do so often it becomes easy. Basically, it's a behavior that you keep repeating. If you persist on at developing a new behavior, eventually it becomes automatic.

Let's look at it this way.

Remember when you learned how to drive? At first it seems very hard, difficult. Perhaps, for some people even impossible. But once you get behind the wheel, as you start to practice your fear starts to fade away. You do it over and over until it becomes easy right?

Everything at first seems hard and difficult, until you learn how to do it and it becomes easy.

Rough commute today?

© CREATIVE MEDIA SERVICES   Box 5955   Berkeley, Ca. 94705

Now, let's go a little further, what about when you drive a standard transmission. If you learn to drive a car with a standard transmission, at first you are probably somewhat nervous right? You've never done it. One of the biggest challenges is trying to coordinate the clutch and the gas pedal, so you can have a smooth gear change (otherwise, you'll look like APOLLO 13, "Houston, we've got a problem.") However, after some practice, and time, it becomes part of you and you don't think about it anymore.

You just created a new pattern.

We go through our life creating sets of habits that in the end will create the life we want to live. We create these habits unconsciously. You might don't know but these habits are the things that are holding you back in life, so STOP blaming others for your failures.

"The results of your bad habits usually don't show up until much later in life."

Many people are living for immediate gratification. They buy things they can't afford right now, putting off payments as far down the road as possible.

Negative habits breed negative consequences. Successful habits create positive rewards. Like it or not, *that's just the way life works*.

If you constantly exceed your income and you spend more than you make, the ultimate outcome for that bad habit will be BANKRUPTCY! You might not like it, but if you keep repeating a bad habit, that's what you will get. Serious consequences.

In the other hand, if you start creating successful habit, your rewards will be pleasurable.

If you want to live longer, you have to change your habits to create good healthy ones. Exercise at least 3 times a week, eat healthy, and even read material that will help you develop that successful habit (Books, magazines, etc)

Developing Successful habits takes time. Don't expect a change to happen overnight, or next week. Give it time and be very disciplined about it.

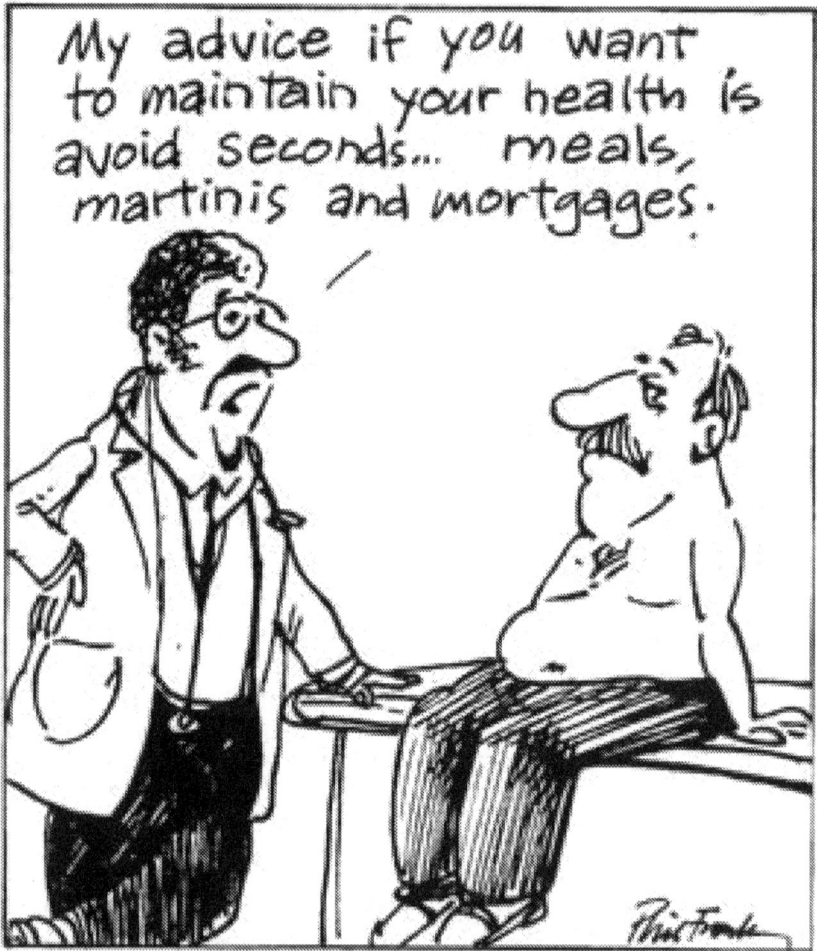

IDENTIFY YOUR BAD HABITS.

I will give you few bad habits that you are probably conscious of right away.

-Not returning phone calls on time.
-Being late for meetings and appointments.
-Having your cell phone ON all the time.
-Answering the telephone during family mealtimes.
-Handling the mail more than once
-Snoozing the alarm too many times before getting out of bed.

These are just few of many bad habits.

Check yourself out by making a list of all the habits that keep you unproductive and not moving towards your goals. Take an hour or more so you can really think through this process. Plan your hour ahead of time so you won't be interrupted.

You can also ask for feedback. Talk to people you respect and admire, who knows you well. Ask them what they observe about your bad habits. What you are looking for here, is consistency. What do I mean by that, if you talk to 10 people and 8 of them tell you that you are always late to meetings, pay attention, it's a clue that will help you get a start.

THE OUTWARD BEHAVIOR IS THE TRUTH, WHEREAS YOUR INNER PERCEPTION OF YOUR BEHAVIOR IS OFTEN AN ILLUSION.

Don't make the same mistake, if you have identified a bad habit, do everything you can to change it.

You can turn negative consequences into positive rewards,
Simply By Changing Your Habits Now.

CHANGING YOUR BAD HABITS.

You might think that changing a habit is difficult, stressful, and almost impossible right?

Wrong.

What if I tell you that it takes about "twenty-one days" or "three to four weeks." Great news isn't?

Now you can feel less pressure when changing your bad habits.

Successful people know that habits will determine your future. Learn to observe those bad habits; it will help you create new ones that will work for you.

A short story I want to share with you, and maybe some of you will relate to, was that I was terrible at waking up. I snoozed the alarm like 30 times before getting out of bed. To realize that I was already late.

I had to rush to the restroom, take a shower if time permitted it, couldn't eat breakfast, caught traffic every morning, late to work, etc. I mean you name it, I had it. It was terrible.

All because of one bad habit.

I had to do something about it, I hated it. Always rushing everywhere because I didn't know how to control and change my habits.

Of course change wasn't easy, especially when it required me to get up earlier, but I had no choice it was that or keep living the same old way, "Always Rushing."

I stopped keeping my alarm clock next to my bed, I moved it across the room, that way I have to get up to turn it off.

I set it up with the annoying BUZZ, because sometimes the radio kept me dreaming.

Then I had my wife holding me accountable to make sure I started waking up. If I didn't wake up, I had my last resource. MY WIFE WILL KICK ME OUT OF BED. You can be sure that that worked really good. It only took one time for her to wake me up and I was GOOD!!!

The greatest thing was that after twenty-one to thirty times of repeating the new habit, it's harder not to do it that to do it.

Once a new habit has been developed, it becomes your new normal behavior.

If other people can develop significant changes, why not you? I have told you before, nothing will change until your do. Start creating new successful habits that will give you more freedom and peace of mind.

Life is a learning experience, and every successful person that you talk to will tell you so. Always strive to improve, that will help you build character.

Study successful people and pay attention to their habits, that can be a great help to start developing a new pattern.

Remember…

"If you keep doing what you've been doing, you will keep getting what you've been getting."

THE SUCCESS THREE FORMULA.

Let me give you a step by step formula to help you create better habits. This formula is simple, to keep your mind at ease, it does not require any calculations nor secret magic nor complicated strategies. You can also apply this method to any area of your life which you would like to improve you habits on.

1. IDENTIFY YOUR BAD HABITS

Earlier in the book I told you about identifying your habits, write them down, and ask people whom you respect and admire for feedback. If you are not aware of your bad habits, look for consistency in your feedback, that will help you analyze what other people see in you. Don't fight it back, instead be open minded and accept the criticism, it's for your own benefit.

When you look at you bad habits or behavior, it may not look so bad, don't get fooled by that, it might not look so bad, but look at it in the long term. For example a smoker will say "What's wrong with few cigarettes a day? It helps me relax and relief some stress." However, twenty years from now when he is in the doctor's office, he will find an ugly picture of his lungs in the X-rays.

Just consider this, if you smoke five cigarettes a day for twenty years, that's a total of thirty six thousand five hundred cigarettes. Do you think thirty six thousand five hundred cigarettes will have an impact in your lungs? In fact, the consequences could lead you to a deadly end.

When you examine your own bad habits, consider the long-term consequences. **Be honest with yourself, you can control your future right now.**

2. CHOOSE YOU NEW SUCCESSFUL HABIT

This is simple, it's just the opposite of your bad habit. To motivate your self, think about the benefits and rewards by adopting your new habit. The more vividly you describe the benefits, the more likely you are to take action.

Think about the smoker, if he stops smoking right now, and change that bad habit for one that is healthy, think about the benefits, for once he will live longer, he will experience less or no health problems in the future, and why not!! You will have extra money in your pocket each month.

Can you see now, that by focusing on the rewards, can be very motivating and exciting.

3. CREATE AN ACTION PLAN

Ok here is where it gets exciting, you need to start by helping yourself, start reading about a specific topic to develop your new habit, use hypnotherapy, and have a friend or a family member hold you accountable. The important thing here is to make a decision about what actions you are going to take.

Stay away from other smokers, use a nicotine patch, you can even place a bet with a friend to keep you accountable. The important thing is that you create an action plan and that you follow it like if your life depended on it. It could be that one day it will.

Once again, remember, nothing will change until you do.

So what are you waiting for. Get a piece of paper and a pencil and start identifying your bad habits, and create you action plan.

Use this template to help you get a start.

My Bad Habits

1. *Snooze alarm clock too many times*
2. *Don't return phone calls on time*
3._____
4._____
5._____

My New Successful Habit

1. *Wake up early*
2. *Return phone calls as promised*
3._____
4._____
5._____

My Action Plan

1. *Put my alarm clock away from my bed*
2. *Set a reminder on my phone and write it down in a paper, and put the paper where I can see it to return phone calls*
3._____
4._____
5._____

You can use the example above to guide you on your habit changing process, I will put a clean template at the end of the e-book, so you can use it over and over.

TAKING ACTION.

"Without action, there will be no results...."
-Jorge Fernandez de Cordova

Are you the kind who like to put things off?

Do you leave everything at the last minute?

For example, you know you need to pay the bills at least 5 days before the due date, but instead you wait until the day before or the due date. Now you have to pay extra to make a rush payment, you stress, your family gets pulled into your mess, creating more anxiety. Somehow you manage to get it done, and you say to yourself "I will never do that again," and what happens next month? You repeat the same thing over again, don't you? Why?

Well, it's your habit of waiting until the last minute. Come on let's face it. You are a procrastinator.

Let me tell you that just about everyone procrastinates, sometimes that's good, and most of the times is bad. Successful people do procrastinate as well, the difference is they know how to manage their time, and they make time to procrastinate.

Not everything in life is work and study. There's more to life than just that, and once in a while you need to take a break.

I'm a big believer that if you work hard, you must play hard as well.

But, how do you get rid of procrastination?

Learning to manage procrastination, is what separated the weak from the strong, the timid from the courageous, and the talkers from the doers.

When we were little we always manage to find activities that kept us busy, and our procrastination level was at is all time low. As we grow up, we develop that bad habit to the max. We let procrastination rule us.

We become the people of tomorrow.

"I will finish the report tomorrow, I will get that done tomorrow, I will buy it tomorrow, etc, etc." And the list just keeps on going.

Let me share with you're the procrastinators creed written by Ed Foreman.

Procrastinator Creed

"Someday when I grow up, finish school and get a job, I'll start living my life the way I want… someday after the mortgage is paid off, the finances are on track and the kids are grown up, I'll drive that new car and take exciting trips abroad… someday, now that I'm about to retire, I'll buy that beautiful motor home and travel across this great country, and see all there is to see… someday."

-Ed Foreman

Our life is wasted by the someday thoughts. Why not take action today, and start achieving those goals instead of whishing and hoping, those two words are excuses for not doing.

Many people lives wanting things, they keep saying to themselves. When I retire, I'm going to be more relax, when I paid my mortgage I will have more money to save, when I become financially independent, I'm going to start living my dream life.

The biggest mistake here is expecting to have things, in order to be more relax, living your dream life, saving more money. Why not do it now?

I will tell you why? You might not like it, but the truth is that you get comfortable with conformity. As long as you have enough, you think you are ok, and without doing anything, you expect things to take care of it's own.

Sorry to tell you that is not true. If YOU don't take action, no one will do it for you, and not a single thing will improve for much you hope or wish for.

Change starts with you.

If you want to stop smoking, you have to be willing to change and most of all recognize you have a smoking problem. The same goes for

We allow smoking in the workplace... ..as long as you don't exhale!

© CREATIVE MEDIA SERVICES   Box 5955   Berkeley, Ca. 94705

drinking and procrastination.

If you really want to become successful, you have to recognize that you have a procrastination problem, and be willing to change.

Stop living in the someday, and start living in the NOW! If you want a new car, instead of saying "when I buy a new car I will travel around with my family…" change it for, "I will travel with my family until I buy my new car…" and create a plan of action to buy that car, you can create a savings plan to achieve that goal. Do the same thing for any goal you want to achieve.

WHEN YOU GET MOMENTUM REMAIN FOCUS.

"The key to success is to **focus** our conscious mind on things we desire not things we fear."
-Brian Tracy

Your focus has to be like a train in a railroad track. You are the conductor, and there's only one way to get from point A to point B.

You go through life like a train go through different places, the speed doesn't really matter as long as you get to your destination. Of course the faster the better, but you have to have a plan and follow it.

I want you to remember those times when you were a little kid and you really wanted that toy (bicycle, doll, car, etc) remember. Where was your focus at all times? You had to go to school, do your homework, you went out and play with your friends, but you always had in your mind the picture of that toy.

As an adult, your focus has to be even greater or at least the same. That will give you the motivation you need to continue on your road to success. You will also experience down times, when you will feel bored, and if your enthusiasm is fading away. Thinking and focusing to end result will help you get to the end.

Don't make the same mistake most people do. You focus so much on the end result, that you forget to enjoy the ride there. Life is a learning experience and as such you have to enjoy every moment of it, because once is gone, it will never come back.

Celebrate your little achievements on your road to destiny. When you finally arrived at your destination or your ultimate goal, the feeling of achievement will be so powerful and worth the trip.

In the other hand if you don't enjoy the process, once you get there, you will be just like if nothing happened.

When you are faced with a challenge, don't quit or give up on your goal. Do as every successful people do. They become problem solvers.

How do you become a problem solver? Right now in your life, you might be a complainer when a challenge arises. Why? That's because your level of awareness and your current habits, do not support you in that field.

Think about the first time you got a flat tire, and you didn't know how to change it. You were probably frustrated, complaining about the last person who used your car, or fixed your car, and you think everything turn into a complete mess.

Now think the same scenario, but this time you have the knowledge to change a tire. This time you might be a little upset about the situation, but you can handle it right? You take out the hydraulic jack, the spare tire, the cross wrench and get to work. Now it's fixed, right?

When you are faced with a challenge, it might not be exactly as changing a tire, and you might not even know how to develop that habit. I want you to do this right now if you are facing any challenge right now.

I'm going to give you the Problem Solver Mind Builder.

This tool will help you get in the habit of training your mind to work for you, to help you create a mind that's solution oriented rather than complaint maker.

I want you to write down in a piece of paper, the challenge you are facing. Ready? Next I want you to write below that challenge, ten possible solutions to fix that challenge.

For example,

My Challenge

I'm late on my bills for this month.

My Solutions

1. *Rush a payment to make it on time,*
2. *Set up automatic payment*
3. *Write the date of the day I have to send the payment on my calendar.*
4. *Etc.*

What you are doing with this exercise, is train your mind to think in solutions instead of complaints.

I want you to do this every time you are faced with a challenge or a problem.

I will put a blank template at the bottom of this e-book as well to help you grow and build your road towards success.

THE NEW YOU.

As you change your bad habits, beliefs, stay focus and become a solution oriented person, the successful you will emerge.

You will be a person of power, direction and planned action.
You will overcome false beliefs which have been holding your success back.
You will be open to new concepts, values and beliefs.
You will have a healthy and longer life.
You will learn to love yourself and others more intensely that you ever have before.

This sounds like a bright picture right? Sure it is, it's the view of the new YOU.

Once you applied the principles contained in this e-book, you will awaken the new YOU. This will required some commitment on your part, you must be willing to sacrifice something to achieve your success, there's no such thing as something for nothing.

This commitment to action will be the greatest adventure of your life. Once you commit and start achieving your goals, you will never be the same again.

THE SUCCESS THREE FORMULA TEMPLATE

My Bad Habits

1. _____
2. _____
3. _____
4. _____
5. _____

My New Successful Habit

1. _____
2. _____
3. _____
4. _____
5. _____

My Action Plan

1. _____
2. _____
3. _____
4. _____
5. _____

PROBLEM SOLVER MIND BUILDER TEMPLATE

My Challenge

_____

_____

_____

_____

_____

_____

My Solutions

1. _____

2. _____

3. _____

4. _____

5. _____

6. _____

7. _____

8. _____

9. _____

10. _____

LAST WORD

I have created this e-book just for you, I want to see each one of you succeed.

I want everyone to grow and be better, better parents, better husbands, better friends, better persons.

I have learned that the best way to help somebody is by being on TOP. What do I mean by that? Let me tell you a short story to explain what I mean.

A guy named Joe was camping with his family, and one day he took his 2 kids for a walk in the Forrest. His children were 4 and 5 years old.

While walking around they fell in a deep ditch. Joe ran to check if his kids were ok. After he checked them, he started to figure out a plan to get everyone out of the ditch.

At first it seem easy, he tried pushing his kids up, and tried to get them out of the ditch and then he will figure the way out himself.

It was a very difficult plan. He couldn't push his kids far enough to where they could get out.

He then tries a different plan, but it required him to be willing to leave his kids alone for couple of minutes.

He told his kids, "Let's play a game, while you guys play, I will find the way out." They agreed and Joe took off leaving his 4 and 5 year old by themselves in the middle of this Forrest.

Pretty scary, but Joe knew that it was the only way to get them out. After 5 minutes amazingly enough, Joe made it to the top, rush looking for his kids inside the ditch, and the kids were very relax playing what their dad had left them playing.

Joe now standing on top, figure out a better plan to extend his hand down and have his kids reached him. Once they reached his hand, Joe was able to pull them up and out of the ditch.

At that moment Joe had learned the most important lesson of his life.

He learned that the best way to help somebody out from a problem, it was a lot easier to be on top and pull them up to were he was, than trying to push them up, which it was harder and it was not a pretty sight.

If you really want to help somebody NOW you know that the best way is for you to be on top and pull people to your level. Instead of you being the step for everyone to climb up.

For your Success,
Jorge Fernandez de Cordova

For Testimonials or Comments

Please write us at:

Support@successismylife.com

Or visit our website at

www.successismylife.com